WHAT WORKS IN
FACILITATING INTERDISCIPLINARY LEARNING
IN SCIENCE AND MATHEMATICS

SUMMARY REPORT

PROJECT
KALEIDOSCOPE

Association
of American
Colleges and
Universities

Association of American Colleges and Universities

1818 R Street, NW, Washington, DC 20009

ISBN 978-0-9827850-2-7

To order additional copies of this publication or to learn about other AAC&U publications, visit **www.aacu.org**, e-mail **pub_desk@aacu.org**, or call **202.387.3760.**

TABLE OF CONTENTS

Acknowledgments

The Keck/PKAL project team would like to thank everyone who has been involved in this project, especially the visionary leadership of Jeanne Narum, PKAL's founding director, as well as the collaborative leadership of Stephanie Pfirman, who helped launch the project, and Michael Kerchner, who has been a coleader throughout the entire project. We are grateful for the generous support of the W. M. Keck Foundation, whose grant made the project possible. There were also many advisors along the way, who helped shape and guide the project through its various phases. We also thank our external evaluators—Adrianna Kezar and Shannon Gilmartin—for their keen observations and insights into the institutional issues surrounding transformational change and longevity of interdisciplinary programs. We also thank the project staff Christina Shute, Jennifer Luebbert, and Kathryn Angeles, as well as other advisors, including AAC&U President Carol Geary Schneider, and Shelley Johnson Carey and Darbi Bossman for their editorial and production assistance. In addition, we want to acknowledge the more than three hundred faculty members and campus leaders who were engaged in the meetings and events associated with the project since 2007.

We are particularly grateful to the teams and campus leaders from the participating campuses:

Agnes Scott College
Beloit College
Bradley University
Canisius College
College of St. Benedict and St. John's University
Davidson College
DePauw University
Florida A&M University
George Mason University
Grinnell College
Indiana University at Bloomington
Jacksonville University
James Madison University
Lafayette College
Moravian College
Nazareth College of Rochester
New York City College of Technology
North Carolina A&T State University
St. Lawrence University
SUNY Oneonta
The Ohio State University
Union College
United States Military Academy
University of Richmond
Wabash College
West Virginia University
Whittier College
Willamette University

◆ LETTER FROM THE EXECUTIVE DIRECTOR

As Project Kaleidoscope (PKAL) approaches its twentieth anniversary, this summary report, *What Works in Facilitating Interdisciplinary Learning in Science and Mathematics,* comes at an opportune time. It is a synthesis of the results from the Keck/PKAL Facilitating Interdisciplinary Learning project that engaged twenty-eight campus teams around the country. Both the project and this report celebrate the PKAL's work over the past twenty years and anticipate PKAL's future, now in partnership with the Association of American Colleges and Universities (AAC&U).

The Keck/PKAL Facilitating Interdisciplinary Learning project began in 2007, following conversations between Jeanne Narum (founding director of PKAL) with colleagues at the W. M. Keck Foundation about current challenges and opportunities facing leaders on undergraduate colleges and universities and about PKAL's potential role in addressing them. It quickly became clear that interdisciplinary learning poses both a challenge and an opportunity, and that an investment by Keck in the work of PKAL would advance what we know about facilitating interdisciplinary learning. This work was intended as a bookend project to another Keck-supported initiative, Facilitating Interdisciplinary Research, undertaken earlier by a task force of the National Academies of Science. Their report focused primarily on the research environment in the university setting. The Keck/PKAL project was envisioned to go more deeply into the undergraduate setting to explore—from the experience of a select group of diverse campus teams—what it takes to create, implement, measure, and sustain effective interdisciplinary STEM (science, technology, engineering, and mathematics) learning environments. Not only are these issues of relevance for STEM higher education, but for the broader community of college and university educators as we strive to graduate citizens and practitioners of science who are well-equipped to engage with and solve this century's pressing challenges.

In this summary report, key recommendations are made and detailed, supplemented by identified strategies and practical advice from the twenty-eight campus teams who were engaged throughout the three-year project. At a culminating national colloquium, over one hundred higher education leaders—either beginning the process of planning for interdisciplinary learning or evaluating or revising existing programs—gathered to hear about, comment on, and contribute to this project from their perspectives. This summary report also contains an initial synthesis of the colloquium feedback. A final report, which will include case studies from campus projects to highlight specific strategies and approaches regarding "*what works,*" is being written and will be available in fall 2011. Details from the project can be found at: http://www.aacu.org/pkal/interdisciplinarylearning/index.cfm.

Looking forward,

Susan Elrod, Executive Director
Project Kaleidoscope
Association of American Colleges and Universities

The Keck/PKAL project was envisioned to go more deeply into the undergraduate setting to explore—from the experience of a select group of diverse campus teams—what it takes to create, implement, measure, and sustain effective interdisciplinary STEM (science, technology, engineering, and mathematics) learning environments."

◆ INTRODUCTION

Interdisciplinary learning is a twenty-first-century imperative. We are continually faced with societal and global challenges that require interdisciplinary thinking to identify suitable solutions, such as finding new energy sources, dealing with the effects of our changing climate, and ensuring populations across the globe have adequate food and healthy living environments. In addition, research in the STEM (science, technology, engineering, and mathematics) disciplines is increasingly crossing traditional disciplinary lines with scientists and engineers collaborating in both basic and applied research projects. In a 2009 report from the National Academies, *A New Biology for the 21st Century*, the interdisciplinary and integrative nature of the biological sciences is described with respect to issues related to global food, health, environment, and energy challenges. This report follows on the heels of others from the National Academies, such as the 2004 report *Facilitating Interdisciplinary Research*, which outlined specific strategies for making research environments more conducive to collaboration. Thus, all college graduates— STEM majors as well as nonmajors—must be able to traverse the complexities of our interdisciplinary and integrated world effectively.

In order to identify specific strategies for facilitating interdisciplinary learning, teams from twenty-eight colleges and universities—representing the diversity of higher education in this country—participated in the PKAL Facilitating Interdisciplinary Learning initiative funded by the W. M. Keck Foundation. During the course of the project, over three hundred faculty and campus leaders were engaged, participating in five national meetings, including two roundtables focused on assessment and leadership. Teams were chosen based on their vision for and commitment to an interdisciplinary learning project; most teams were at the beginning of a process for creating a new interdisciplinary program or facility on their campus (campus project titles are found in Appendix A). Teams were surveyed at the beginning and the end of the project regarding institutional structures, barriers, climate, and other issues. Teams submitted annual reports as formative measures of progress. The recommendations and strategies in this draft report were drawn from conversations at institutes and roundtables, as well as from final team reports submitted in July 2010.

> **Interdisciplinary thinking is rapidly becoming an integral feature of the research as a result of four powerful "drivers:" the inherent complexity of nature and society, the desire to explore problems and questions that are not confined to a single discipline, the need to solve societal problems….students, especially undergraduates, are strongly attracted to interdisciplinary courses, especially those of societal relevance."**
>
> —National Academy of Sciences. 2004. *Facilitating Interdisciplinary Research.*

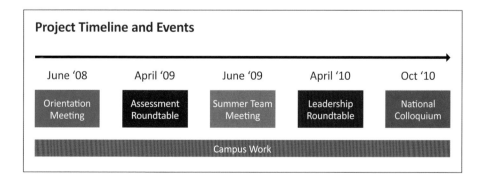

Project Timeline and Events

June '08	April '09	June '09	April '10	Oct '10
Orientation Meeting	Assessment Roundtable	Summer Team Meeting	Leadership Roundtable	National Colloquium

Campus Work

"

The essence of the New Biology is integration— re-integration of the many subdisciplines of biology, and the integration into biology of physicists, chemists, computer scientists, engineers, and mathematicians to create a research community with the capacity to tackle a broad range of scientific and societal problems."

—National Academy of Sciences. 2009. *A New Biology for the 21st Century.*

The projects undertaken by the Keck/PKAL teams ranged from infusing interdisciplinary STEM into general education and first-year experience programs to shaping interdisciplinary courses in teacher education and majors programs in environmental science, neuroscience, and human biology. The campus teams' work culminated in drafting recommendations, defining successful strategies, and spotlighting practical advice in three key areas:

- leadership: facilitating institutional change
- learning: developing goals and intended outcomes for interdisciplinary learning programs
- campus culture: building and sustaining interdisclipinary programs.

This executive summary report outlines five key recommendations with specific strategies and practical advice from the experience of the campus teams involved in the project:

1. Start by articulating a common understanding of STEM interdisciplinary learning goals that will drive the cycle of curricular innovation, development, assessment, and improvement.

2. Use assessment to connect interdisciplinary learning goals with program structure, content, and pedagogy, paying attention to students as individual learners, who come with diverse backgrounds, experiences and expectations, career aspirations, and goals.

3. Build a critical of mass of faculty, from within and with new hires, that assumes leadership responsibility in the iterative process of shaping interdisciplinary curricular and cocurricular approaches and in assessing the impact of those approaches on undergraduate STEM learners.

4. Incorporate interdisciplinary program needs into the processes of campus governance and resource distribution—financial, personnel, equipment, and spaces.

5. Align interdisciplinary learning with the institutional vision, mission, and identity, as well as in strategic planning processes at all levels.

While most campus projects focused on STEM discipline courses and programs, several also included the arts and humanities; therefore, the recommendations presented here are broad in scope. In addition, this report contains feedback received from a broader higher education audience in attendance at the October 2010 national colloquium. A complete report, which will include case studies from campus projects to highlight specific strategies and approaches regarding *"what works"* is being written and will be available in spring 2011. Details from the project can be found at: http://www.aacu.org/ pkal/interdisciplinarylearning/index.cfm.

Student learning is the central activity of science education and must be the first concern of those wishing to improve it. If students learn well, other responsibilities such as the good of the nation, the scientific pipeline, the mission of the institution, and the quality of teaching will be faithfully discharged (PKAL 1991).

Vision and Dimensions of Interdisciplinary Learning in Fields of Science, Technology, Engineering, and Mathematics

Our vision of the student engaged with a robust interdisciplinary learning environment, adapted from the National Research Council (NRC) report *Facilitating Interdisciplinary Research* (2004), is that she or he:

- is able to solve problems that draw on multiple disciplines and able to seamlessly integrate information, data techniques, tools, perspectives, concepts, and/or theories from two or more disciplines or bodies of specialized knowledge to advance fundamental understanding to solve problems whose solutions are beyond the scope of a single discipline or area of research practice
- understands the inherent complexity of nature and society; has the desire to explore societal problems and questions that are not confined to a single discipline, and recognizes the need to solve problems

This NRC vision mirrors PKAL's driving vision of a student-centered learning environment (1991), one in which:

- learning is personally meaningful to students and faculty, makes connections to other fields of inquiry, embedded in the context of its own history and rationale, and suggests practical applications related to the experience of students

Our goal is the cultivation of students who understand the inherent complexity of nature and society, have the desire to explore problems and questions that are not confined to a single discipline, and recognize the need to solve problems whose solutions are beyond the scope of a single discipline or area of research practice. This requires that students are able to solve problems that draw on multiple disciplines and seamlessly integrate multiple perspectives by integrating information, data techniques, tools, concepts and/or theories from two or more disciplines or bodies of specialized knowledge in ways that advance fundamental understandings and/or practical solutions.

This vision for interdisciplinary learning is supported by an institutional culture in which there is clear and documented evidence that students are intentionally *engaged as integrative learners*, gaining skills and confidence in working at the interface, and dissolving the boundaries between disciplines or making them more porous in exploring and addressing societal problems and research questions. This culture is characterized by visible leadership that ensures the intellectual, social, operational, and physical infrastructures required to facilitate long-term interdisciplinary learning. It is a culture in which all students, no matter their background and career aspiration, are motivated to pursue learning experiences that turn them into interdisciplinary thinkers.

A word cloud of this report

◆ LEADERSHIP: FACILITATING INSTITUTIONAL CHANGE

At the Spring Keck/PKAL 2010 Leadership Roundtable, participants defined that leaders must:

- clearly communicate a rationale and vision for undergraduate interdisciplinary learning that is both nationally and locally relevant
- be knowledgeable about models and strategies for facilitating undergraduate interdisciplinary learning in their local context; understand that it is a developmental process and be able to deal with both negative and positive outcomes as the process unfolds
- know when success has been achieved, then reward and celebrate it

It should come as no surprise that leadership plays a critical role in facilitating interdisciplinary learning. As the project came to a close, we sought broader input on recommendations and strategies that leaders should consider. Leaders in this context are grassroots student and faculty activists working to create interdisciplinary programs, and formal campus leaders who make decisions and move important institutional levers. Leaders with responsibility for the quality of interdisciplinary STEM learning also include those in disciplinary societies, accreditation agencies, private foundations, and industry. We want to stress that leadership within each of these levels and communities is essential if a shared vision for interdisciplinary learning and for success in sustaining interdisciplinary programs is to be realized.

Three critical strategies for successfully and sustainably undertaking the recommendations in this draft report are: (1) start with broad and inclusive conversations, and keep them going; (2) engage both grassroots activists and institutional champions in working together toward shared goals; and (3) establish a culture of evaluation, reflection, and continuous improvement.

One of the trickier aspects of leadership for interdisciplinary learning is being able to acknowledge and embrace the necessary tension between the "bottom up" and "top down" leadership of the campus. Both are important and each can support the other in different ways. For example, the dean, provost, and/or president can give credence and validity to division/college/campus discussions regarding interdisciplinary learning by sanctioning and attending the meetings. Faculty can lead by documenting and disseminating program successes, raising grant or other external funding, and realizing campus priorities through interdisciplinary learning courses, programs, and projects. Campus leaders have a responsibility to involve faculty leaders in a collaborative way, and faculty leaders have a responsibility to communicate project/program progress to campus leaders. Obtaining buy-in from the middle layer of the institutional leadership structure (department chairs, deans) may be the most difficult. They need to be engaged early in the conversation. Ultimately, an interdisciplinary program's success and sustainability will depend upon how well it addresses the needs of all STEM students, as well as the institution as a whole. Therefore, students must be included as partners in the formative process of program development.

◆ LEARNING: DEVELOPING GOALS AND INTENDED OUTCOMES FOR INTERDISCIPLINARY LEARNING PROGRAMS

Specific learning objectives, distilled from campus reports and conversations at project meetings, set the stage for discussing the recommendations, strategies, and practical advice that will inform ongoing work—within and beyond the Keck/PKAL community—to facilitate interdisciplinary learning, nurture interdisciplinary integrative thinkers in undergraduate learning communities across the country. As was noted in discussions at the national colloquium, many of these learning objectives are common to all undergraduate programs, and taken together, embody the outcomes of a liberal education for the twenty-first century such as those described in AAC&U's Liberal Education and America's Promise campaign. Liberal Education and America's Promise (LEAP) is a national initiative of the Association of American Colleges & Universities (AAC&U) to champion the importance of a twenty-first-century liberal education, for individual students and for a nation dependent on economic creativity and democratic vitality. Through LEAP, hundreds of campuses are making far-reaching educational changes to help all their students—whatever their chosen field of study—achieve a set of essential learning outcomes fostered through liberal education. In numerous LEAP projects and activities, AAC&U partners with institutions and state systems as they make these essential learning outcomes a framework for educational excellence.

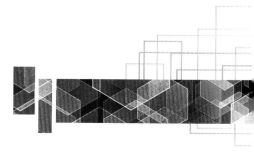

LEAP ESSENTIAL LEARNING OUTCOMES

Knowledge of Human Cultures and the Physical and Natural World
- Through study in the sciences and mathematics, social sciences, humanities, histories, languages, and the arts

Intellectual and Practical Skills, Including
- Inquiry and analysis
- Critical and creative thinking
- Written and oral communication
- Quantitative literacy
- Information literacy
- Teamwork and problem solving

Personal and Social Responsibility, Including
- Civic knowledge and engagement—local and global
- Intercultural knowledge and competence
- Ethical reasoning and action
- Foundations and skills for lifelong learning

Integrative and Applied Learning, Including
- Synthesis and advanced accomplishment across general and specialized studies

Association of American Colleges and Universities. 2007. *College Learning for the New Global Century.*

Jacksonville University

The learning objectives that emerged from the work of campus teams are as follows. As the result of intentional interdisciplinary learning experiences, students will be able to:

- Recognize disciplinary strengths, process, limitations, and perspectives.
- Purposefully connect and integrate knowledge and skills from across disciplines to solve problems.
- Synthesize and transfer knowledge across disciplinary boundaries, even beyond the STEM disciplines, in the context of novel situations.
- Be agile, flexible, reflective thinkers who are comfortable with complexity and uncertainty, and can apply their knowledge to respond appropriately and positively.
- Understand that other factors—cultural, political, ethical, historical, and economic—must be considered when addressing the complex problems of this century.
- Understand the universal nature and deep structure of science, as well as the relationship of STEM disciplines to other disciplines.
- Prepare for future learning as lifelong learners in their careers and as citizens.
- Apply their capacity as integrative thinkers to solve problems in ethically and social responsible ways.
- Think critically, communicate effectively, and work collaboratively with others within diverse cultures and communities.

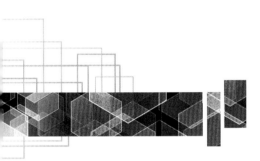

LEARNING GOALS FROM LAFAYETTE COLLEGE

1. Students will have an exceptional educational foundation in the natural sciences, humanities, social sciences, and engineering in the context of life, the earth, and the environment. This includes, but is not limited to, historical information, the scientific process, scientific literacy, and ethics.

2. Students will acquire skills necessary to integrate information from the natural sciences, humanities, social sciences, and engineering related to life, the earth, and the environment. Students will come to understand the growing importance of interaction among scientists, engineers, physicians, humanists, and policy makers. This includes, but is not limited to, using problem-based learning experiences to examine problems from multiple perspectives and solve problems using multiple approaches.

3. Students will be trained and given opportunities to express themselves through a range of communication skills. Thus, graduates will have the skills necessary to be active participants in initiating and promoting change related to life, the earth, and the environment.

◆ CAMPUS CULTURE: BUILDING AND SUSTAINING INTERDISCIPLINARY PROGRAMS

The graphic below illustrates the three main steps in the process of building and sustaining interdisciplinary programs, as informed by the work of this project's campus teams as well as work by Kezar and Lester (2009).

It begins with *mobilizing* a team of faculty and campus leaders to plan the program or project. Critical steps at this stage are defining the interdisciplinary vision and goals (including specific student learning outcomes); knowing the institutional context (including student interest, faculty expertise, local opportunities, funding opportunities, etc); and providing an experimental space for idea generation and the testing of new ideas. Communication, inclusiveness across disciplines, and transparency of process are important factors during this stage, which can take from three to twelve months or more.

Once planned, programs are *implemented*, starting small with pilot programs that are tied to deliberate assessment methods that will measure the initial success and point to places for improvement and scale-up. The process of piloting, evaluating, and scaling can take from one to three years, depending on campus culture, resources (including faculty and funding), and institutional context and readiness. These first two stages are also facilitated by the infusion of external funding. It is in these two stages where campuses usually spend most of their time.

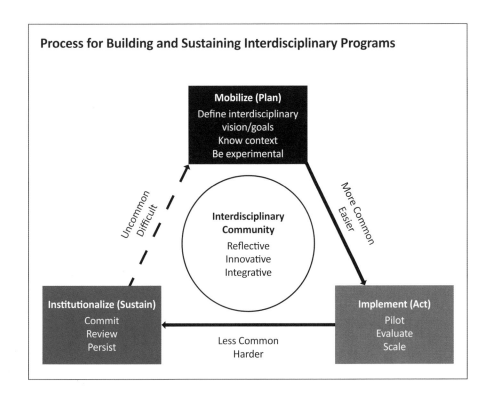

Process for Building and Sustaining Interdisciplinary Programs

> **Student learning is the central activity of science education and must be the first concern of those wishing to improve it. If students learn well, other responsibilities such as the good of the nation, the scientific pipeline, the mission of the institution, and the quality of teaching will be faithfully discharged."**
>
> —Project Kaleidoscope. 1991. *What Works: Building Natural Science Communities.*

The final stage, *institutionalization*, is the most difficult. Fewer of the campuses participating in this project were at this stage in their efforts by the end of the grant period. To achieve this stage, campuses must commit to the program, reviewing the evidence of its success and then refining infrastructure and resource requirements, and persist in supporting it over the long haul. Even in the toughest budget times, campuses can move programs forward—perhaps on a modified time scale—as long as they remain focused. Lastly, we assert that campuses must connect back to their original vision and goals periodically to ensure that programs are meeting their goals. This step in the process may be the most rare, especially given turnover in campus leadership that may shift institutional priorities and plans.

This whole process is mediated by an *interdisciplinary community* of faculty, students, staff, and leaders who employ reflective, innovative, and integrative thinking as they work toward program sustainability. Leadership on campus and from external stakeholder groups is required throughout the process, asserting influence and providing support in different ways along the cycle.

◆ SPECIFIC RECOMMENDATIONS, STRATEGIES, AND PRACTICAL ADVICE

At the heart of interdisciplinarity is communication—the conversations, connections, and combinations that bring new insights to virtually every kind of scientist and engineer."

—National Academy of Sciences. 2004. *Facilitating Interdisciplinary Research.*

Recommendation One—Start by articulating a common understanding of STEM interdisciplinary learning goals that will drive the cycle of curricular innovation, development, assessment, and improvement.

Strategies

- In a timely and appropriate manner, have discussions at various levels about what students should know and be able to do as a result of their undergraduate interdisciplinary learning experiences; keep all stakeholders informed about the process and outcome of those discussions; and connect interdisciplinary learning goals to institutional vision, mission, and strategic plans.
- Solicit and utilize insights from alumni, employers, and other stakeholders about the value-added perceptions of and/or experiences with interdisciplinary learning and learners.
- Use the process of Wiggins and McTighe's *Understanding By Design* (2001) to create plans for new courses and programs.
- Examine current/anticipated curricular and pedagogical approaches to determine relevance/potential to serving established interdisciplinary learning goals.
- Survey existing campus resources/practices for assessing student learning to determine relevance/potential for supporting efforts to facilitate interdisciplinary learning and to aid in institutionalizing interdisciplinary learning.
- Stay informed of national trends, relevant resources, and projects of peers to ensure the latest methods and metrics are being employed, as well as to build from the work of colleagues.
- Use an experimental approach by piloting new programs on small scale, including evaluation, before making major changes. Take small steps in implementation that allow for iterative exploration of new curricular/pedagogical strategies and mechanisms for developing a feedback loop between program planning and assessment.
- Monitor the valued-added aspects of interdisciplinary learning at every step of the process for continuous program improvement and/or phase out programs that are no longer helping students meet desired learning goals, to ensure relevance and efficacy.
- Consider putting interdisciplinary learning in developmental courses so students can see the relevance of science and mathematics even at this early, basic level.
- Remember that it is about the student as learner.

Practical Advice from Campus Teams

- Use both formal and informal campus structures to have conversations and to communicate about interdisciplinary learning—department meetings, committees, research groups, professional development workshops/programs, reading groups, websites, and student organizations. Do a SWOT analysis as part of the planning process—analyze strengths, weaknesses, opportunities, and threats.
- Connect interdisciplinary learning efforts to program review or campuswide accreditation or other initiatives (undergraduate research, planning for new or renovated spaces, service learning) when possible.
- Connect interdisciplinary learning goals to other learning goals—e.g., quantitative reasoning, critical thinking, personal and social responsibility; particular attention must

be paid to the balance between breadth and depth when planning interdisciplinary learning experiences.

- Hire tenure-track faculty in science education with expertise in learning and assessment.
- Include non-STEM faculty and administrators in the conversations to provide broad perspective and gain buy-in from other, possibly unanticipated, corners of the campus.
- Conduct an informal campus survey of faculty, staff, and students to gain broader feedback on program goals and/or activities. Ask students what their goals are and how they think they might be best achieved.
- Send faculty and staff to teaching, learning, and assessment conferences, meetings, and workshops—AAC&U, PKAL, and the Council for Environmental Deans and Directors were mentioned as useful resources for project teams.
- Realize that the first step—setting appropriate and relevant learning goals—takes time (months!), especially across departments, disciplines, and other campus units. Be patient with the process of dialogue and discovery.
- Make the case for interdisciplinary learning in the context of the changing nature of scientific research in the twenty-first century (more interdisciplinary and more focused on addressing real-world problems) as well as workforce development needs.
- Collect student feedback early and often—students are key stakeholders whose opinions should be part of the planning and review process of interdisciplinary programs.
- Don't wait to determine the resources and support needed for program success; think about this from the outset.
- Align student recruitment messages with interdisciplinary programs.
- Invite faculty from other campuses to talk about their programs; organize visits to institutions that have aspirational programs or facilities that include "deep dive" immersion experiences with programs or spaces that promote interdisciplinary learning.

De Pauw University, photographer Steve Woit

Recommendation Two—Use assessment to connect interdisciplinary learning goals with program structure, content, and pedagogy, paying attention to students as individual learners who come with diverse backgrounds, experiences, expectations, career aspirations, and goals.

Strategies

- Accept that assessment is a dynamic and continual process that occurs over time.
- Align assessment methods with interdisciplinary STEM learning outcomes and goals; determine and adapt what works best for your community.
- Use or adapt existing instruments—don't reinvent the wheel—unless absolutely necessary (see box at right).
- Work with colleagues within and beyond the campus to explore, design, and pilot assessment approaches; participate in building a broader, informed community of assessment practitioners, locally and nationally.
- Disseminate results of your assessment within and beyond the campus; document and publicize the impact of your efforts on student learning.
- Integrate interdisciplinary assessment tools and approaches into ongoing campuswide program review, assessment, and accreditation efforts.
- Include students as collaborators in the processes of designing interdisciplinary pedagogies, assessment methods, and curricula.

Practical Advice from Campus Teams

- Be certain to start with well-defined, measurable learning outcomes.
- Take small steps—focus on measuring one learning outcome first, reviewing the data and making improvements on that outcome before attempting to measure and adjust others.
- Use a sampling approach when monitoring populations of students over time. It isn't always necessary to measure the learning of every student all the time.
- Hire/utilize faculty in science education with expertise in learning and assessment.
- Seek external funding to support initial phases of planning and assessment. Once program is up and running, ensure that it becomes institutionalized throughout appropriate campus processes and structures.
- Use an external evaluator to help monitor program progress, when funds and expertise exist.
- Seek collaborations and partnerships with other institutions sharing common programmatic issues or goals; it may also be useful to have comparative programmatic data to inform program improvement.
- Support and reward faculty work in assessing and improving interdisciplinary courses, programs, and student experiences.

Recommendation Three—Build a critical of mass of faculty, from within and with new hires, that assumes leadership responsibility in the iterative process of shaping interdisciplinary curricular and cocurricular approaches and in assessing the impact of those approaches on undergraduate STEM learners.

Strategies

- Seek new faculty lines that target areas of teaching and research at the interface of more than one discipline, in the context of an anticipated interdisciplinary initiative; for campuses with adjunct faculty, hire individuals with industry or other relevant work experiences that will bring the real world closer to students.

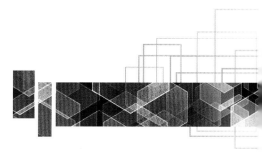

SOME ASSESSMENT INSTRUMENTS REFERENCED IN CAMPUS REPORTS

- National Survey of Student Engagement (NSSE)
- Faculty Survey of Student Engagement (FSSE)
- Collegiate Learning Assessment (CLA)
- Association of American Colleges & Universities (AAC&U) VALUE rubrics
- Summer Undergraduate Research Experiences (SURE), Classroom Undergraduate Research Experiences (CURE), and/or Research on Integrated Science Curriculum (RISC)
- Student Assessment of Learning Gains (SALG)
- Field-Tested Assessment Guide (FLAG)
- Views about Science Survey (VASS)
- Course evaluations/student evaluations of faculty
- Embedded exam questions
- Other institutional data (course/program retention, Higher Education Data Sharing (HEDS))
- Biology Self-Efficacy Scale, Science Literacy Scale, Self-Determination Scale

- Create faculty review, promotion, and tenure policies to recognize and reward faculty efforts toward engaging students in interdisciplinary learning in STEM fields.
- Promote formal and informal conversations (within divisions, through learning/ teaching centers, within campus committees, during retreats) that offer recurring opportunities for collective discussions about the value of interdisciplinary learning for students for whom they have common responsibility.
- Promote formal and informal conversations between interdisciplinary faculty as mentors and advisers with students pursuing and exploring interdisciplinary learning opportunities.
- Provide timely incentives and make targeted support available for interdisciplinary faculty, staff, and students, including funds for travel, program development, and improvement efforts (course release, supplies for initial course offerings, sabbaticals, etc.).
- Incorporate interdisciplinary teaching and assessment strategies in educational training programs for graduate students.

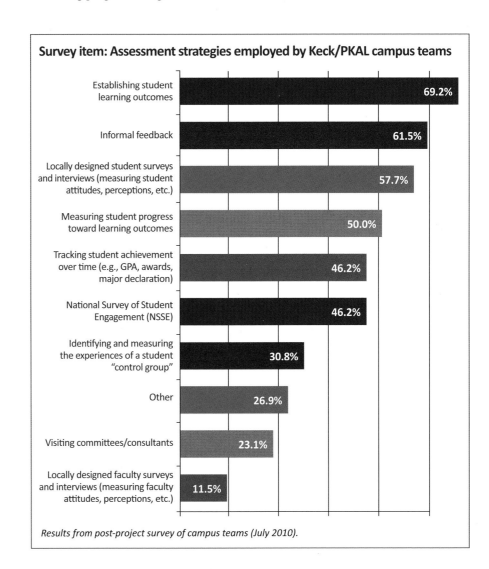

Survey item: Assessment strategies employed by Keck/PKAL campus teams

Establishing student learning outcomes	69.2%
Informal feedback	61.5%
Locally designed student surveys and interviews (measuring student attitudes, perceptions, etc.)	57.7%
Measuring student progress toward learning outcomes	50.0%
Tracking student achievement over time (e.g., GPA, awards, major declaration)	46.2%
National Survey of Student Engagement (NSSE)	46.2%
Identifying and measuring the experiences of a student "control group"	30.8%
Other	26.9%
Visiting committees/consultants	23.1%
Locally designed faculty surveys and interviews (measuring faculty attitudes, perceptions, etc.)	11.5%

Results from post-project survey of campus teams (July 2010).

- Start small and work within campus cultures and environments to create the appropriate level and scope of interdisciplinary learning (e.g., freshman seminars, linked courses, clusters of electives, gateway and capstone courses, and minors).
- Use Council of Environmental Deans and Directors (CEDD) documents on hiring and promoting interdisciplinary faculty.
- Include a phrase about "interest in interdisciplinary programs" in disciplinary job advertisements; include related questions during the interview process.
- Create campus faculty development opportunities to ensure competence in developing, assessing, and teaching in interdisciplinary learning environments; promote faculty learning communities around interdisciplinary learning goals, program planning, and assessment.
- Engage early-career faculty at all levels. They have fresh, relevant ideas and experiences, especially in the research realm.
- Consider the adjacencies of faculty offices and gathering spaces for students; determine if they promote interdisciplinary interactions among faculty and students, and between faculty and students.
- Offer workshops and programs through campus centers for teaching and learning that focus on interdisciplinary learning outcomes and assessment.
- Create and participate in regional networks of campuses or colleagues that leverage experience and expertise to create collaborations around interdisciplinary research and learning environments.

Recommendation Four—Incorporate interdisciplinary program needs into the processes of campus governance and resource distribution—financial, personnel, equipment, and spaces.

Strategies

- Align budgetary structures, allocation, and reallocation procedures to support interdisciplinary programs, faculty, students, and spaces. It isn't always about adding on, but often about redistributing—and the structures for both need to be transparent.
- Align institutional fundraising initiatives, including the search for federal and private agencies, with support for programmatic and institutional goals regarding interdisciplinary learning.
- Integrate efforts to renew, recycle, renovate, and create new learning spaces in the process of making decisions about institutional priorities and budgets.
- Establish formal administrative structures and leadership positions in support of interdisciplinary programs (e.g., Center for Interdisciplinary Studies, dean of Interdisciplinary Studies, Center for Materials Science).

Practical Advice from Campus Teams

- Ensure campus curricular approval and review processes enable the development of interdisciplinary learning courses and programs.
- Create a clearinghouse list of faculty whose appointments are exclusively or partially in interdisciplinary programs.
- Include development staff in planning meetings, or meet with them separately, to ensure interdisciplinary learning and program goals are on the fundraising agenda.
- Repurposing space, faculty lines, resources, and other infrastructures allows institutions to address creatively needs for interdisciplinary learning in ways that aren't additive, which ensures more complete integration into institutional culture.

> ❝
>
> **We overcame most departmental turf barriers by having education research specialists from most the STEM departments on the leadership team along with a central member from the Office of the Dean of research... Co-teaching and course buy-outs were one of the biggest barriers for us that we did not overcome. However, based on success at gaining NSF funding for an interdisciplinary faculty development workshop, we have renewed interest in integration across introductory biology, chemistry and mathematics to a level beyond the scope of our PKAL project.”**
>
> —Keck/PKAL Campus Team 2010 Report

- Overcoming departmental barriers is probably the biggest challenge to interdisciplinary programs—create strategies for addressing these challenges early in the process; don't ignore departments in the process. Include them early on, especially the department chair or other department leaders.
- Ensure interdisciplinary programs have the same rights and responsibilities as disciplinary programs, from approval to program review; ensure that interdisciplinary program faculty and/or directors are present at budget and other institutional planning meetings; create governance documents or memorandums of understanding to make explicit the support of interdisciplinary programs.
- Create/renovate spaces and facilities to promote interdisciplinary learning. New spaces aren't always required—renovations offer an opportunity to consider revised spaces that will facilitate interdisciplinary learning.
- Visibly support interdisciplinary projects with travel funds, meeting space, and course release/reassignment; ensure that formal campus leaders attend interdisciplinary project/program planning meetings
- Support interdisciplinary faculty research alliances and partnerships; create visible mechanisms (funding, spaces, centers).
- Create transparent financial policies, including criteria for how budgets are established and reviewed; align program aims with needed resources.
- Consider mechanisms for ensuring that divisional or campuswide voices are heard in tenure and promotion decisions as they relate to interdisciplinary learning.
- Negotiate or adjust indirect costs from interdisciplinary grants to go to interdisciplinary faculty development or interdisciplinary teaching buy out.

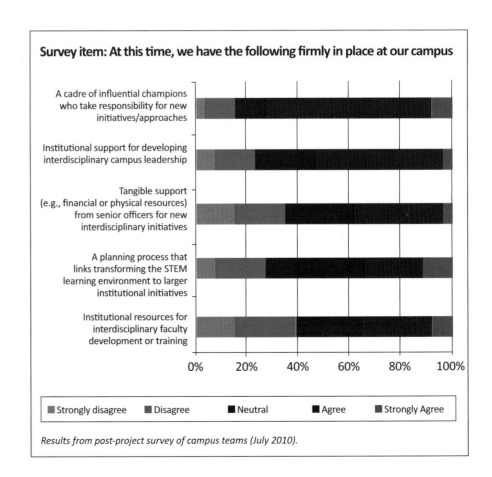

Survey item: At this time, we have the following firmly in place at our campus

Results from post-project survey of campus teams (July 2010).

Survey item: Most challenging institutional barriers

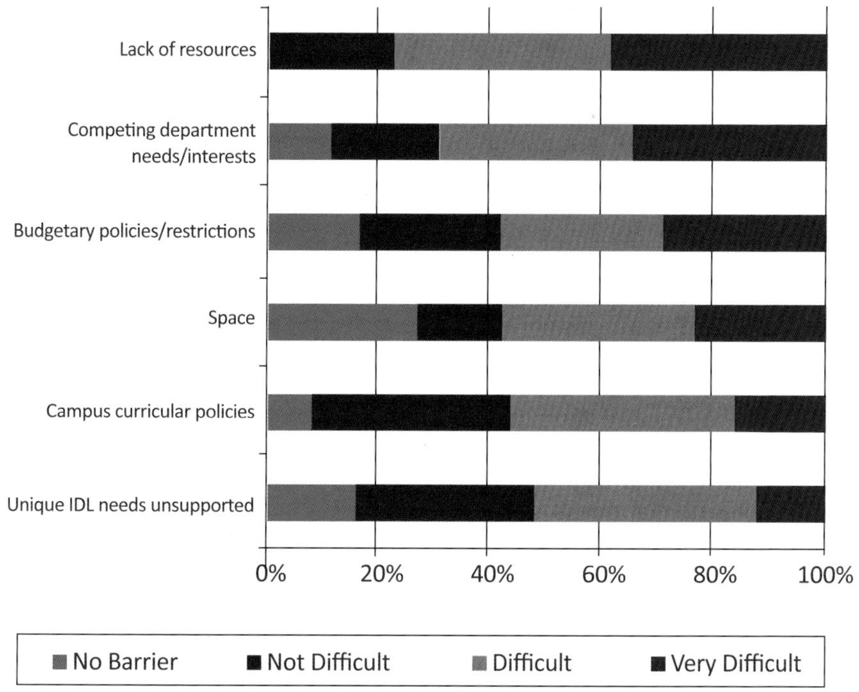
Lack of resources
Competing department needs/interests
Budgetary policies/restrictions
Space
Campus curricular policies
Unique IDL needs unsupported
0%
20%
40%
60%
80%
100%
No Barrier
Not Difficult
Difficult
Very Difficult

Results from post-project survey of campus teams (July 2010).

Recommendation Five—Align interdisciplinary learning with the institutional vision, mission, and identity, as well as in strategic planning processes at all levels.

Strategies

- Identify current area(s) of strongest potential for facilitating interdisciplinary learning, seeking to leverage new programmatic development in terms of student interest and existing interdisciplinary activity through courses, curriculum, and/or faculty research.
- Engage in a campuswide conversation, including students, student affairs, admissions, advancement, facilities, etc., regarding interdisciplinary learning to develop a shared vision; take a holistic view of student learning across the entire experience, inside and outside the classroom; connect interdisciplinary learning goals to campuswide student learning goals.
- Be prepared to negotiate the difficult territory between the cultures of different campus units, departments, divisions, and colleges.
- Create collaborations and partnerships—internal and external—focused on established interdisciplinary learning goals.
- Use students as champions and advocates.
- Educate campus leaders regarding the benefits and value of interdisciplinary learning in the context of the campus mission as well as the goals for students and faculty; engage in the difficult conversations about the process of change and transformation.
- Celebrate achievement of key interdisciplinary milestones and successes.

> "[C]ollaboration is extremely difficult because not only are our organizations based on principles and structures antithetical to collaboration, so are our larger systems of government, foundations, disciplinary societies, and the like. So, the challenges exist within all parts of the system. Leaders … will be more successful encouraging collaboration if they can acknowledge their own challenges in collaborating, learn from these experiences, and try to be role models for higher education—a system that is even more embedded in an ethic that prevents collaboration."

—Adrienne Kezar and Jamie Lester. 2009. *Organizing Higher Education for Collaboration*

Practical Advice from Campus Teams

- Start with targeted, strategic areas of science that relate to emerging research or industry trends (nanotechnology, sustainability, climate science).
- A focus on global education may enable interdisciplinary learning in STEM, and bring in other disciplines for broader campus participation.
- Consider general education as a place to develop and implement interdisciplinary learning in STEM (and beyond); leverage existing general education committee and review processes in support of interdisciplinary learning.
- Make interdisciplinary goals explicit in accreditation plans and reports.
- Ensure teams have cross-disciplinary representation, as well as administrative representation.
- Be prepared to talk openly about the disciplinary "territory" issues, and create mechanisms for dealing openly with them.
- Pay deliberate attention to the development and support of emerging campus leaders with interdisciplinary vision, interests, and responsibilities.
- Leverage existing program or research strengths to foster interdisciplinary learning (e.g., marine science program, interdisciplinary research center, service learning program). Take advantage of opportunities in the local community to create interdisciplinary programs (e.g., study of a complex bioregion, environmental cleanup site, community organizations).

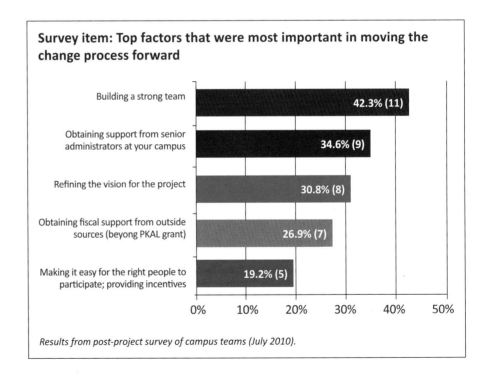

Survey item: Top factors that were most important in moving the change process forward

Building a strong team	42.3% (11)
Obtaining support from senior administrators at your campus	34.6% (9)
Refining the vision for the project	30.8% (8)
Obtaining fiscal support from outside sources (beyong PKAL grant)	26.9% (7)
Making it easy for the right people to participate; providing incentives	19.2% (5)

Results from post-project survey of campus teams (July 2010).

◆ ACTIONS EXTERNAL STAKEHOLDERS CAN TAKE TO HELP ADVANCE INTERDISCIPLINARY LEARNING

At the national colloquium, participants considered how the following constituent groups could take proactive measures to advance interdisciplinary learning on campuses:

- institutions of higher education (IHEs), all types from community and technical colleges to large, public research universities
- funding agencies and organizations, both public and private
- higher education associations, such as accreditation organizations, member associations, and assessment institutes
- scientific disciplinary societies

The actions recommended for IHEs largely reflected the recommendations in this report, and where they differed, new ideas were incorporated in this summary report.

For the other three categories, which make up a critical group of external constituents, a synthesis of recommendations from the colloquium is shown in the table below. However, all external constituent groups should consider the following recommendations in order to help facilitate and advance interdisciplinary learning:

- Develop a common understanding and language within the organization for what interdisciplinary learning means; formalize the language, value, and urgency of interdisciplinary learning.
- Review organizational practices, policies, publications, and programs through the lens of interdisciplinary learning; triangulate that review with strategic goals with respect to the audience(s) served by the organization (including students!).
- Look for, highlight, and promote best practices of interdisciplinary learning—programs, assessment methods, institutional practices, hiring, promotion, and tenure, etc.—from the organization's perspective and capitalizing upon the use of organizational websites, publications, electronic communications, and other communication and media outlets.
- Work toward establishing more interorganization conversations, conferences, publications, and projects that would allow interactions between and among the disciplines and members with the goal of increasing cross-disciplinary collaboration and communication.
- Host national conferences and workshops on interdisciplinary education programs, assessment, research, and institutional change, perhaps engaging the community through regional consortia and conferences; include researchers, educators, and students in these meetings.
- Another key external constituent group is industry. In many cases, colleges and universities are already partnering with local and national industry partners through cooperative programs and internships, research collaborations, and industry advisory boards. Some institutions have created truly collaborative spaces that industry and students share. Encouraging these kinds of interactions is exactly what is needed to bring the real world closer to students in order to put into practice the kind of educational experiences we know work well.

Recommendations from the Colloquium

Funding Agencies and Organizations	Higher Education Associations	Disciplinary Societies
• Strengthen the peer-review process to better accommodate interdisciplinary proposals—reviewers may need additional training in interdisciplinary learning, assessment, and institutional change • Pay careful attention to interdisciplinary learning and outreach activities of interdisciplinary research programs • Support multimonth think tanks for discipline-based faculty and educational researchers to develop interdisciplinary research projects and programs • Consider mechanisms to support programs that take on the challenges of institutional transformation and change in the context of interdisciplinary learning	• Continue synthesis, publication, and research on best practices for interdisciplinary learning to reach national audiences • Provide more guidance on leadership for institutional transformation and change • Create guidelines within accreditation frameworks, including learning outcomes and assessment practices • Create interdisciplinary learning assessment items for national assessment instruments and surveys • Incorporate issues of interdisciplinary learning, assessment, and change in higher education leadership programs	• Utilize national conferences as a way to highlight interdisciplinary topics—both research and learning; hold joint society meetings around cross-disciplinary research and learning; and include K–12 professional organizations • Provide more access of discipline-based education journal articles to an audience beyond membership of the organization • Publish special issues of journals that highlight interdisciplinary research and teaching • Provide professional development workshops that focus explicitly on interdisciplinary teaching, learning, and assessment • Create awards that recognize interdisciplinary educational teaching and programs

◆ REFLECTIONS FROM PKAL'S PAST

The recommendations in this draft summary report are consistent with and reminiscent of PKAL's previous Leadership Initiative project. A synthesis of insights from that earlier project found that *what works* is:

- openness to change, signaled by presidential vision and action that is evident in many ways
- a sense of long-term stability with decisions made collectively and thoughtfully about each next step and new direction in the context of the institutional culture and mission, and where that approach to decision-making has contributed to a culture of trust
- intentional weaving by leaders of a "tapestry of change," in some instances taking small steps and in others pursuing breathtaking and timely new initiatives
- persistent attention to what students are learning and to the process of learning and teaching
- visible evidence that "everyone is on board" in thinking about student learning—from facilities managers to library directors to assessment officers to faculty in all disciplines
- visible evidence that the campus is intentional and sophisticated in identifying and adapting relevant work of peers, in order to be most efficient in regard to time and funds in the work of reform

◆ REFERENCES

Association of American Colleges and Universities. 2007. *College Learning for the New Global Century.* Washington, DC: Association of American Colleges and Universities.

Kezar, Adrianna, and Jamie Lester. 2009. *Organizing Higher Education for Collaboration: A Guide for Campus Leaders.* San Francisco: Jossey-Bass.

National Academy of Sciences. 2004. *Facilitating Interdisciplinary Research.* Washington, DC: National Academies Press.

National Academy of Sciences. 2009. *A New Biology for the 21st Century.* Washington, DC: National Academies Press.

Project Kaleidoscope. 1991. *What Works: Building Natural Science Communities.* Washington, DC: Project Kaleidoscope.

Wiggins, Grant, and Jay McTighe. 2001. *Understanding by Design.* Englewood Cliffs, NJ: Prentice Hall.

Appendix A. Titles of Keck/PKAL Campus Projects

Campus	Project Title
Agnes Scott College	*Problem-Solving across the Sciences*
Beloit College	*Supporting Interdisciplinary Majors at Beloit College: Curriculum, Assessment and Institutional support*
Bradley University	*Interdisciplinary STEM Education for All*
Canisius College	*Mission-centered Programmatic Development and Implementation for Science Hall*
College of St. Benedict and St. John's University	*Integrative Science for the 21st Century*
Davidson College	*Aligning Strategic Planning and Facilitating Interdisclipinary Learning*
DePauw University	*Integrating Environmental Studies into the Liberal Arts Experience*
Florida A&M University	*STEM Learning Community at Florida A&M University*
George Mason University	*Towards a Conservation, Environmental and Sustainability Issues General Education Requirement*
Grinnell College	*Developing Interdisciplinary Courses/Assessing Interdisciplinary Learning*
Indiana University at Bloomington	*Promising Practices for Facilitating and Sustaining Interdisciplinary Learning*
Jacksonville University	*Learning Communities: STEM and Beyond—Global Environment, Local Solutions*
James Madison University	*Implementing and Facilitating Interdisciplinary Programs*
Lafayette College	*Facilitating Interdisclipinary Learning in Health and Life Sciences*
Moravian College	*Toward a Truly Interdisciplinary Environmental Science Program*
Nazareth College of Rochester	*Facilitating New Interdisciplinary Initiatives at Nazareth College*
New York City College of Technology	*Creating and Sustaining an Interdisciplinary STEM Culture at City Tech*
North Carolina A&T State University	*Integrating General and Major Science Education*
St. Lawrence University	*Math Support Center as ID Catalyst*
SUNY Oneonta	*Use of Common Case Studies in Multiple Courses to Enhance Interdisciplinary Learning and Environmental Problem Solving*
The Ohio State University	*Ohio's Science and Engineering Talent Expansion Project (OSTEP)*
Union College	*Integrating Environmental Science, Policy and Engineering (ESPE)*
United States Military Academy	*Facilitating Interdisciplinary Learning Project*
University of Richmond	*Integrative Quantitative Science at University of Richmond*
Wabash College	*Examining Opportunities for Interdisciplinary Teaching and Learning in Biochemistry and Biophysics*
West Virginia University	*"VARIETY at WVU"—Vision At Reaching Interdisciplinary Experience Training for Youth at West Virginia University*
Whittier College	*Establishing Interdisciplinary Centers*
Willamette University	*iScience: A Pedagogical Framework for Promoting Science Literacy*